FOREWORD

Seventy years ago the 'Penn Bus Company' started its first service from Tylers Green to Beaconsfield Station. At that time many roads were inadequate for motor vehicles and many others were impassable because they were too narrow or too steep for the mechanical abilities of those early buses. For the next fifteen years the Company was part of a transport revolution in the High Wycombe district which not only improved but appreciably changed the lifestyle of the average country dweller that it served, whose only means of transport until then was the pedal cycle.

In 1920 there were very few restrictions governing such a business and, with fierce competition and rivalry, the success that it achieved was due to its loyal hard-working staff, and also to its faithful and hard-won customers. My father, Frederick James Sugg was well known for his toughness and determination and his disdain for the idle employee. Yet, even as a strong disciplinarian he was fair and considerate to those who were prepared to work hard. As his son I was subjected to the same discipline, even when I was made Manager. He was obsessive about time-keeping and insisted that all conductors carried watches. Those starting work at the age of 14 years could not afford them, so a watch would be issued on a pay by instalment basis. When the Company was sold, he, at the age of 76 was in the garage at 5 a.m. to ensure that the buses left promptly for the last time.

In this detailed and well-researched history, Paul Lacey provides a worthy and lasting record of 'The Penn Bus Company', its machinery and its employees.

Francis J Sugg, 1990

1

Acknowledgements

Information and photographs for this book have been gleaned from a number of sources, many of them with direct connections to the old 'Penn' company. I would like to thank everybody who has given me assistance with this project, no matter how small their contribution; but particular thanks go to the following individuals and organisations-

The Bucks Free Press, Mrs Jessie Clarke, Dick Cuff, the Guildford Muniments Room, Arnold Highfield, the late Joe Higham, the Reference Section of High Wycombe Library, Mr & Mrs Kilminster, The Omnibus Society, John Parke, John Proffit, the PSV Circle, Reg Westgate and Peter Wilks. It was also most pleasing to be able to interview Francis Sugg and to gain an insight into day-to-day life at 'Penn'.

Wokingham   *January 1990*

Published by Paul Lacey, 17 Sparrow Close, Woosehill, Wokingham, Berkshire, RG11 2UQ

110 01

Other titles by the author (available from the above address - trade and society enquiries welcome):-

The Independent Bus & Coach Operators of the Newbury Area, 1919 - 1932   £4.95 + 25p P&P

A History of Newbury & District Motor Services Ltd., 1932 - 1952   £6.75 + 50p P&P

2

When Frederick James Sugg moved to the Buckinghamshire village of Tylers Green in 1913 he envisaged a life of semi-retirement after a working life of hard toil.

Never a man who was at ease when doing nothing, he inevitably involved himself in a number of activities - but even he could not have foreseen that he would duly become the owner of the largest and best remembered bus operation in the High Wycombe area.

Born near Wells in Somerset in 1859, he had left school to work on the land at the age of 8. When he was 17 he took some further schooling to enable him to read and write and thereafter moved to London. He was a tough and determined man, whose skills at navvying led to him operating gangs of men on a variety of tasks including the digging the first tunnel for an underground railway beneath the Thames. He had a particular knack of sizing up the requirements of a job and then the tenacity to see it through.

Frederick Sugg saved his money up until he had enough to buy a ton of coal and then set about establishing what was to become a substantial coal merchants business. At first he hawked the coal himself from a horse and cart, but other members of his growing family later joined him as the Highgate-based business expanded.

During that time his wife passed away, he remarried and the family moved to Barnet by 1911, when the last child of the second marriage (Francis) was born. The Highgate business continued for many years in the care of his son Charlie and grandson Walter, latterly becoming motorised, and a pig farm was also started in Hertfordshire.

Frederick's second wife Alice had originated from the High Wycome area, and it was therefore to that area that they looked when he decided to become semi-retired following a serious illness.

At Tylers Green Mr Sugg bought land in St Johns Road, where he built a house called Woodside View, but it was after the end of the First World War that certain events led him to become involved in public transport.

There had been an established horse bus service between Tylers Green and Beaconsfield Station before the end of the war, but after peace returned a couple of local men started to run a motor taxi over that route. They soon found themselves in some financial strait and approached Frederick Sugg for assistance. However, after thinking it over he decided that he could do better by running a larger vehicle on that route. He therefore did not join with them, instead setting off to the war surplus vehicle sales at Slough in search of a chassis for his new venture. An Austin 2-tonner was obtained and sent to Coles & Co. of High Wycombe for the fitting of a bus body.

The completed vehicle returned to him at the end of January 1920 and had seats for 20 passengers, with 9 longitudinal seats each side of the body and a further 2 beside the driver. Its chassis had some unusual features, such as the radiator being mounted at the rear of the engine ('coal scuttle' arrangement as it is sometimes called), whilst the drive was by individual shafts to each rear wheel. Solid tyres were fitted all round and the passenger entrance was at the extreme rear, whereas lighting was by oil for the side-lamps and acetelyne for the head-lights.

A former chauffeur named Piercey was taken on to drive the bus and Frederick Sugg acted as conductor. 9-year old Francis accompanied Piercey when he went to collect the vehicle from Coles and he would also work as a conductor in his holidays and weekends until taking it up on a full-time basis when he reached 15. Driver Piercey is recalled as being somewhat nervous of his charge due to its poor braking going down hills and the difficulty of engaging low gear when travelling up hill.

The Austin was registered as BH 0311 on the 27th January 1920 and the service between Tylers Green and Beaconsfield Station commenced on 5th February. 5 journeys per day were run, but the main objective was to provide transport for passengers who wished to take the trains to and from London.

Indeed, commuter housing had built up in the area known as Beaconsfield New Town, whilst grander houses were also to be found along the route. Later during the morning there were the ladies who wished to shop in London, but the early morning runs were for the business types and the bus would always stop outside the gate of those regulars, one of whom was Lord Dawson of Penn.

As the service was tied to the train timetable, strict punctuality was required to reach the station in time for outgoing trains, whereas the bus would always wait for homecoming trains whenever they were delayed.

The service did indeed soon justify itself, although the Austin was dogged with mechanical problems related to its complicated drive arrangement.

In order that the service could be maintained at all times a second vehicle was obtained and Coles were asked to provide a 14-seat rear entrance body for it. The chassis was a Ford 'Model T' and it was duly registered on 3rd July 1920 as BH 5951. Its arrival took Frederick Sugg out of the realms of the one-bus operator and onto a pathway that was to see the business continue to expand every year for the next 15.

With the arrival of the Ford it soon became apparent that it would be a good idea to find some additional work for the small 'fleet'. Prior to 1920 it had been common for the Tylers Green folk to walk the 5 miles or so into High Wycombe across country through Kings Wood. The advent of the 'London General' service betwen Uxbridge and High Wycombe had provided a link from the main road at Wycombe Marsh, but on the homeward journey that still left the wearisome walk back up to the village.

About August 1920 Frederick Sugg began to run a Fridays-only market day trip into High Wycombe. It proved to be a very popular facility and gave shoppers a 2-hour stay in Wycombe - the bus laying over at the Frogmoor Gardens until the return trip. Whilst waiting at that very spot one Friday, something occurred which was to cause Mr Sugg to consider further expansion of his bus services. He had, of course, already noted that the 'Thames Valley' buses, which had taken over on behalf of the 'General' on the Uxbridge route in 1922, were filled up by the Inspector calling for the longer-distance passengers first - this always leaving the more local passengers at a disadvantage when the buses were busy.

Then one day, whilst Frederick Sugg was waiting with his bus at Frogmoor, he was approached by a group of women who had completed their shopping in Wycombe but had been left behind by the 'Thames Valley' bus. They asked him if he would hire them his bus to take them home to the Wycombe Marsh area and, having time still to spare, he readily agreed to take them.

At first the service to the Marsh may have only been a market-days facility, but a further 1-ton Ford was soon fitted out with a 14-seat rear entrance body by Coles and placed on the road in August 1922. Its registration number may have been BH 9409 (but this remains unconfirmed) and its arrival made it possible to commence regular daily operations between Wycombe (Frogmoor) and Wycombe Marsh. Such an act placed Sugg in direct conflict with 'Thames Valley', but his neat and nippy Fords could easily out-pace the 'Valley's heavy Thornycrofts and the service therefore prospered.

5

A third Ford of similar layout etc. joined the fray in March 1923 (believed to be registered BH 9991) and the drivers Ted Bryant and Cyril Meadows kept up the pressure to ensure that the little buses were both full and fast! With this additional bus it was possible to intensify the service and also to extend it eastwards to Loudwater and to West Wycombe at the western end. This also increased hostility with 'Thames Valley' as it took away further passengers from the Uxbridge route and also from the Wycombe to Maidenhead service which ran by way of Loudwater.

Indeed, the 'Valley' had high hopes of expansion for itself in the Wycombe area and made temporary arrangements to rent a shed at the paper mills at Loudwater in September 1923 in order to provide a more local base for its buses until plans could be approved for a proper garage in the town. As soon as the Loudwater shed was organised, they set about their expansion with new routes from Wycombe to Great Missenden and to Holmer Green and Penn (via Terriers and Hazlemere). The latter route was clearly inaugurated in order to fight Sugg on his own ground!

Whether Frederick Sugg had thought of any title for his bus venture at the outset is unclear, but it soon became referred to as the 'Tylers Green & Beaconsfield Bus service'. This description became somewhat inadequate after 1922 and the name 'Penn Bus Company' evidently came into use during the early months of 1923. The livery from the outset was a medium shade of green together with some cream (or broken white), though the proportions varied with body styles.

To return to the services, Frederick Sugg now found himself locked in earnest competition with 'Thames Valley', and rather than being put down by this it actually made him all the more determined to expand! The 'Valley' had beaten him to the Great Missenden route, but undeterred, he ordered up a new bus specifically to start his own service over that route.

The bus duly arrived and was licenced PP 1194 on 15th January 1924. Based on the Dennis 2 1/2 tonner goods chassis it was given a 26-seater rear entrance body by Strachan & Brown of Acton and took up its duties on the 'Missenden route in the care of driver George Honeyman. This first Dennis had the distinction of being the first bus in the little fleet to be allocated a fleet number (No. 1), but the other existing buses were not given any such numbers. It also heralded a new era in passenger comfort, being the first bus of its size in the Wycombe area to have pneumatic tyres all round.

A second Dennis of the same type and bodywork followed in July 1924 and became No. 2 (PP 2245), being used to provide an improved service on the Wycombe to Penn route in the care of driver George Knowles. Its arrival allowed one of the little Fords to be put on a new service from Frogmoor out to the expanding housing estates at Desborough Park Road.

Loadings on the Loudwater to West Wycombe route had by then become too much for the Fords to cope with, so some larger buses were ordered to take their place on that service. Again, they were Strachan & Brown 26-seat rear entrance buses built on the Dennis 2 1/2 ton model and, as 'Penn' Nos. 3 and 4 they were registered PP 3006 and PP 3005 (respectively) on Christmas Day 1924.

Both Nos. 3 and 4 were put onto the West Wycombe to Loudwater route with effect from 1st January 1925, the service actually being extended in the east from Loudwater to Wooburn Green (thereby following the 'Thames Valley' route even further towards Maidenhead!).

The displaced Fords were soon found other work - one went onto the Desborough Park Road route, allowing the service to be both improved in frequency and onwards into the evenings, whilst the other was earmarked to pioneer yet another new route.

This additional venture also commenced on New Year's Day 1925 and ran from High Wycome to the village of Speen via the Hughenden Valley and North Dean. Prior to that a local builder named Ward had used his lorry (fitted with benches) to run into Wycombe on Fridays, but the advent of the 'Penn' service soon saw the demise of that.

To run up to Speen was indeed a bold venture, considering the hills encountered and the narrowness and condition of some of the road traversed.

Although all 'Penn' buses were washed every day at the end of their work, the dust (in Summer) or mud (in Winter) of the mainly un-tarred roads often left them looking chalky or mud-splattered during the day, although a curtain inside the rear protected the passengers. Conductors were expected to ride on the rear platform when not actively collecting fares, and they often looked like flour-millers after a dusty run out to the hill villages!

However, the expansion of the 'Penn' operations was not without its difficulties, and these came three-fold. Firstly, the Chief Constable Mr W T Jones had been delegated the task of issuing hackney carriage licences in the Borough of Chepping Wycombe, and he took a particular interest in the increasing bus traffic. Mr Sugg never made any effort to keep himself on the right side of Jones, which left 'Thames Valley' the relatively easy task of presenting its own activities as more 'respectable' than those of 'Penn'. In reality, the crews of both firms infringed against the Chief Constable's rules quite equally, but he seemed less quick to condemn the 'Valley' itself. Secondly, the Council had for some time been growing concerned about the traffic congestion at the Frogmoor Gardens, and had therefore come up with a scheme to relocate some of the operators elsewhere (in Queen Victoria Road). 'Penn' were, however, allowed to stay put at Frogmore following a worrying time when it looked as though their routes would be split between the two termini.

The third, and indeed most pressing, problem besetting 'Penn' at that time was an acute shortage of drivers in the area. To overcome that matter Frederick Sugg invited some men up from Hindon in Wiltshire (through local connections he had there), and in that way was able to recruit 5 drivers (Jack 'Gypsy' Smith, Dick Cuff, Ron Stone, Garnet Dunford and another), a conductor Harry Snooks - who later went onto driving - and a greaser, Colin Horner, who later drove for the LPTB.

Another local lad, Clement 'Felix' Allman, was employed as a conductor and became known as a character on the 'Penn' by his ability to step off a bus at 10-15 m.p.h. facing the opposite direction of travel! He also had a rather large head and had to have a cap made specially to suit him.

'Thames Valley' were still, however, determined to expand in the Wycombe area, and they demonstrated that by opening a new purpose-built bus garage at Wycombe Marsh in August 1924 - thereby once again bringing further intensity to the competition between the two concerns.

1925 brought further improvements to frequencies on the 'Penn' routes as three further Dennis's of the same type and bodywork were added to the fleet in April (No. 5, PP 3811), September (No. 7, PP 4875) and December (No. 8, PP 5166).

Also delivered during July 1925 was No. 6 (PP 4616), which was a special little 16-seater built on a Dennis 30 cwt. chassis to be used

8

on a new route to Naphill via the narrow road from Bradenham. Its body had forward-facing seats in pairs on one side of a central gangway and single seats on the other side and the entrance was at the rear. The body was very much a scaled-down version of those previously built on the larger Dennis's and was once again a Strachan & Brown product. No. 6 took up its alloted duty on the new service which ran by way of West Wycombe (Pedestal) and then on to Bradenham and up to Naphill.

It should be noted that it was the Company's practice to put conductors on all of its buses at that time - including even No. 6 and the 14-seater Fords - the idea being to leave the driver free to concentrate on driving the bus and keeping it ahead of the 'Valley bus! Indeed, although timetables did appear for services from time to time, it was Frederick Sugg's usual comment to say that his buses ran '2 minutes in front of the 'Thames Valley' ones!'

He was also a very particular man, and would sometimes supplement the efforts of his appointed Inspector by doing some spot-checks out on the road himself (Hazlemere crossroads, watch in hand, was one of his favourite places), and woebetide any drivers not running on time. He was also sometimes known to go into the 'Blue Tea Room' at Frogmoor to remind crews that they were due out on the road! However, when all is said and done, he was actually quite kindly to those who served him well, often arranging for accommodation for crews.

Promotional opportunities at 'Penn' were also based on employees performance and reliability - drivers had to prove they could handle the vehicles well and conductors had to be trustworthy with the takings. At first new crews would be put on the shorter local runs along the Wye Valley floor, where it was easier for the Inspectors to keep an eye on them, before being sent out farther afield. A degree of personal rivalry was actively fostered by Frederick Sugg in order to get his employees to drum up trade in a effort to out-do each other. In particular they were expected to enter wholeheartedly into the competition with the 'Thames Valley' crews.

Once Mr Sugg felt he could really trust a driver he would assign him to 'the hills' routes, where his skill at handling the bus would be tested daily. With conductors, promotion meant the routes where more cash was taken in. Of the latter, Arnold Highfield was a good example of how trust could be repaid. He joined the Company as a 15-year old conductor in November 1926 and rose to become an

Inspector at just 17. He credits his swift rise to the events of a particularly busy Saturday night, when the last bus to Penn was jam-packed with passengers coming home from Wycombe (as many as 55 being carried on a 26-seater!). As was the custom, he had remained on the rear platform whilst the bus climbed up Amersham Hill (in case of a roll back should the bus stall - wooden chocks being carried on all the buses), but even afterwards he found it quite impossible to move amongst the crowd to collect the fares. The only thing to do was to take the fares as the people left the bus, but quite a few passengers did not wait for their tickets. The following morning he was summonded to the office to explain to Mr Sugg how it was that his takings exceeded his ticket sales. Once he had recalled the situation of the night before, he was praised for his honesty and then duly awarded the post of Inspector when a vacancy arose. The original Inspector had been Jimmy James (also helped in the office with the 'books'), his place being taken by a Mr Ward(?). Arnold Highfield followed him, whilst in later years the position was held by Jack Hobbs who went onto the LPTB and rose to be a 'Gold Badge' Inspector.

The 'Penn' Inspector also had a special responsibility to ensure that the buses were not sent out on 'the hills' routes when ice was present. It therefore fell to Inspector Highfield to make early-morning tours of the most notorious spots (e.g. Missenden Hill, Cryers Hill, Treadaway Hill, and the most feared Amersham Hill) before the first buses were due out on days when icy conditions threatened. Arnold recalls that there were rather too many occasions when he (and his motorcycle) discovered the ice on the road the hard way! Prior to Highfield's appointment, it had fallen to Francis Sugg to be awoken by the Night Foreman at 3 a.m. on those occasions to take out the 'Bullnose' Morris for such inspections - the 'dickie-seat' being loaded down to improve traction.

Most of the time though, the Inspector was based at the Branch Office at No. 35 Frogmoor, which had come into use by 1926 and was situated overlooking the bus stands. This proved particularly useful as the garage and Head Office remained some 5 miles away at Tylers Green.

Indeed, the distance between the Frogmoor stands and the garage could have lead to a considerable amount of dead mileage, but special consideration was given to ensure that buses coming off routes at Wycombe were used to run journeys in service to Penn, Tylers Green or to Totteridge or Loudwater as part of their homeward run. On

10

Friday and Saturday nights any such buses were lined up at Frogmoor to await the mass exodus from the cinemas.

At the other end of the scale, the potentially wasted mileage of running an early-morning positioning journey from Wycombe to Great Missenden was avoided by sending the bus cross-country via Terriers and Four Ashes to take up the service route into 'Missenden at Great Kingshill (the reverse arrangement occurring each evening).

As the Austin had proven itself to be mechanically unreliable it saw less and less use as the fleet expanded, and it was replaced on the Beaconsfield Station route by the first of the Chevrolets in 1926.

Francis Sugg had, in the meantime, attended commercial classes at the Technical School in High Wycombe and was able to audit the Company's accounts at the age of 14! He had of course continued to work as an occasional conductor until he left school at 15, when he went onto 'Penn' fulltime from September 1926. Francis's natural inclination was to have sought a career elsewhere (being a wireless operator on a ship took his fancy at the time), but once he was fully involved with the buses he was expected to tackle any tasks put his way in the same way that his father had always done.

With the expansion of the routes out to the hill villages, a parcels service duly came about and a number of parcel agents were arranged. These varied in their character with the location and were amongst others, 'Samways' at Great Missenden, the publicans at Speen, North Dean and Naphill and the 'Stores' at Walters Ash. Conductors issued appropriate value Bell Punch tickets as receipts and the parcels could either be dropped off at the nearest agent or met en route. At the Wycombe end all parcels traffic was dealt with at the Frogmoor office. Carying work was not generally undertaken - though the description of 'parcel' was widely interpreted in those days. Another regular job involved one of the little Fords which, prior to taking up its daily duties on the Desborough Park Road service would make an early-morning trip to Wycombe Station to collect bundles of newspapers for distribution to Popp's at Frogmoor and several other newsagents in the town centre.

It should be noted that relations with other local bus operators were always kept on a good footing, the competitive zeal being ranged against 'Thames Valley' by all the locals rather than fighting between themselves. This did, however, tend to restrict the development of 'Penn' operations mainly to the north, east and south-east of Wycombe (see Route Map, Centre pages).

11

Both Frederick and Francis Sugg were keen Salvationists, so no Sunday services were run in the early years. However, public demand was duly met in that respect.

As already mentioned, the Frogmoor office was very much the daytime hub of the organisation, and it was also the base for an unusual facet of Frederick Sugg's attention to detail. Not only was he concerned about the external appearance of his buses, but he was also particular as to how they smelt! Workmen all seemingly smoked incessantly in those days, whilst the school children carried on the slightly later trips in the mornings added their own range of aromas to the interiors. Therefore after each morning and evening 'rush' was over, all incoming buses were given a spray inside with a carbolic solution - though this was duly changed to a nicer-smelling lavendar solution - dispensed from garden spray guns.

Competition with 'Thames Valley' continued throughout the mid-1920's and led to a number of complaints being brought before the Council concerning buses racing each other and not running according to the timetables set out or approved by the Chief Constable. The 'Valley' did of course do its bit to bring the competition to the 'Penn' homeground, such as the June 1926 extension of its existing Penn route onto reach Beaconsfield a number of times during the day.

Only two buses joined the 'Penn' fleet during 1926 and they were both replacements for older stock - all other vehicles to date having been additional vehicles required to match expanding operations. One was a further Dennis 2 1/2 tonner with Strachan & Brown 26-seat rear entrance bodywork. This became No. 9 (PP 6811) which, although of similar outward appearance to previous examples had an engine with a larger bore, and replaced the first of the Fords.

The other delivery of 1926 came in September and consisted of a small Chevrolet purchased as a replacement for the Austin on the Beaconsfield Station service. Numbered 10 (PP 6918), it was fitted with a new 14-seat body (believed built by Coles) which had a front entrance in order that the service could be operated on a one-man basis. Loadings on the service during the day could be light but the one-man idea was not used for the other routes. This vehicle remained on that service all the time, in the care of driver Dunford or Woodley.

In the meantime Francis's duties became more varied and he only conducted on occasions. In those days a motorcycle licence could be obtained at 14 and the actual licence was the same document for cars and motorcycles alike - the inappropriate class being deleted when the licence was issued. Francis had already taught himself to drive his fathers Ford T car when he was about 12 years old in the yard at Tylers Green, and he therefore took little prompting to take to the wheel when he discovered that the official had inadvertantly issued him with a licence at age 16 without the 'car' part deleted!

One of his regular duties from about 1926 was the repair of the quite numerous punctures picked up on the flint roads. Such events did not hold the buses up too much, as drivers competed with each other for the fastest wheel change - 8 minutes being the 'record'. Incoming crews would deposit their punctured tyres at the Frogmoor office during the day and take away a sound wheel in its place. The punctures would then be collected up by Francis in the 'dickie-seat' of a 'Bullnose' Morris then assigned as the service vehicle for carrying back to the garage where he would set about effecting repairs. That in itself was not the easiest of tasks with the beaded-rimmed tyres then in use, and Francis and a fitter had many a struggle getting all the repairs done in readiness for the next day.

Whilst engaged on the tyre work Francis also set up 'Wycombe Tyre Service' as a side-line, his regular customers being 'Penn' and the Wycombe chair manufacturers..

Up until then the crews had been issued with reefer jackets or dust coats suitable for summer work as a semblence of uniform. However, on a visit to a tyre manufacturers in Scotland, Francis found himself with time to spare in Glasgow and was most impressed by the smartness of the Corporation Tramway's crews in their uniforms of dark bottle green with yellow piping. On his return he managed to persuade his father of the good public image such garments would ensure, and all of the men to soon kitted out with new made-to-measure uniforms and hats bearing the Company title in brass lettering.

After a spell repairing punctures Francis was 'promoted' to painting the bus roofs with white lead oxide paint, but this had to cease after a bout of lead collic. He then dealt with signwriting the route boards (though fleetnames continued to be done by Mr Halson from Wycombe) and even mastered the skillful art of varnishing repainted buses.

During these times he also continued to look after the accounts with some assistance from a sister who helped out at the Tylers Green office. The only other member of the family involved in the business was Fred Sugg (a nephew of Frederick's) who came up from Sparkford in Somerset, aged 14, and worked as a conductor from September 1927. He later married Vera Goodearl and worked for many years at the well-known Goodearl Bros. Furniture factory.

The next vehicles to come up for replacement were the two Fords which had spent much of their time racing back and forth between Frogmoor and Desborough Park Road. During February 1927 their 14-seater bodies were re-mounted onto new Chevrolet LM-type chassis, and the resultant vehicles became Nos. 11 and 12 (PP 7563 and 7564) before taking up their duties on the busy local service with its 7 minute journey time and 1 penny fare.

Other deliveries for 1927 consisted of two more Dennis 2 1/2 tonners. Their bodies were once again 26-seaters by Strachan & Brown, but unlike previous examples these were front entrance vehicles. They were No. 14 and 15, but a slight dispute with Chepping Wycombe Borough Council concerning the overall length of one of them caused their registration numbers to end up out of sequence, with 15 taking to the road in July as PP 8721 and 14 following in October as PP 9263.

It will of course be noted that there was no Number 13 as that was considered too 'unlucky' a number to bestow upon a vehicle. No. 15 was therefore the thirteenth bus to be delivered since fleet-numbering began, and it was not long before it earned a reputation as the 'bogie bus' of the fleet!

One other delivery also took place at the start of 1927 in the shape of a Dodge car which replaced the old Ford T tourer used on taxi work. That particular aspect of the business had not developed as such, and in due course it faded out altogether - the Dodge then being used as a service vehicle for the fleet. Frederick Sugg had tended to do the odd bits of taxi work himself, but found that he virtually had to relearn how to drive when the Dodge replaced the Ford and its unique 3-pedal system.

On the services front, two new features had been brought in during June 1927. One was the extension of the West Wycombe

14

The 'Penn' fleet
A photographic review

Proud to be part of 'Penn', conductor Arnold Highfield poses for a snap with 'Little Dennis' No. 6 (PP 4616)

This rather fuzzy view is the only one showing one of the three Ford Ts used by 'Penn'. Taken at Queen Victoria Road during the winter of 1926/7, it shows the type of bodies fitted to the extended 'T' chassis and the cutaway rear entrance position.

The Dennis $2^1/2$ tonner formed the backbone of the 'Penn' fleet for many years. All received 26-seater bodies by Strachan & Brown, No. 4 (PP 3005) being a rear-entrance example delivered at the very end of 1924.

Top left: The 'gov'ner'
Frederick Sugg in the
outfit he wore for
conductoring.

Top right: Francis Sugg
prepares to take Gilford
No. 22 on a seaside run.

Bottom: The first Dennis
purchased, No. 1 (PP 1194)
and conductor about to
leave on a Naphill journey

Purchased specifically 'to go where no other buses had dared to go', diminutive 30 cwt. Dennis No. 6 (PP 4616) pioneered several routes to the hill villages during its stay with 'Penn'. The 16-seater body was by Strachan & Brown and was very much a scaled down version of the type fitted to the $2^1/2$-tonners.

Three of the Dennis $2^1/2$-tonners were treated to new 26-seat front entrance bodies at the Wycombe factory in 1928. No. 7 (PP 4875) was one of the trio and is seen on the busy service out to Mill End Road via Desborough Park Road after being rebodied. Note the use of both roller blind and route board displays.

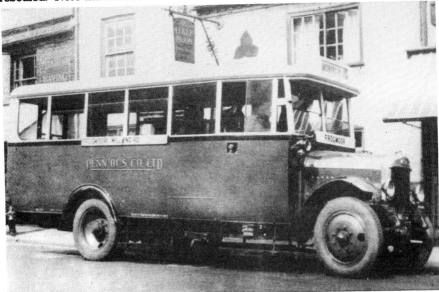

Dennis $2\frac{1}{2}$-tonner No. 9 (PP 6811) leads a line-up of 'Penn' buses at the Frogmoor stands - very much a hub of life in the Wycombe town centre of yesteryear.

No. 15 (PP 8721) enhanced its 'bogie bus' image in this incident with a large tree near Great Kingshill in January 1928. The crew and passengers were very lucky to escape without injury!

The aftermath of No. 15's entanglement with the tree! This view was taken at the Strachan & Brown works before work began on removing the damaged body, parts of which were used to construct a similar replacement.

The combination of the Dennis $2^{1}/_{2}$-tonner and Strachan & Brown bodywork continued to find favour at 'Penn' for a number of years, though the engine design was progressively refined and the choice of entrance position was switched from the rear to the front. No. 14 (PP 9263) was one of two such buses delivered during 1927.

'Penn's' first move to forward-control vehicles came with the purchase of No. 16 (PP 9657), a 1928 example of the Leyland 'Lion' PLSC1 type. Strachan & Brown built the 32-seater body - note the ornate support bracket on the front bulkhead - and No. 16 is believed to have been the first vehicle to have the light green waistrail band.

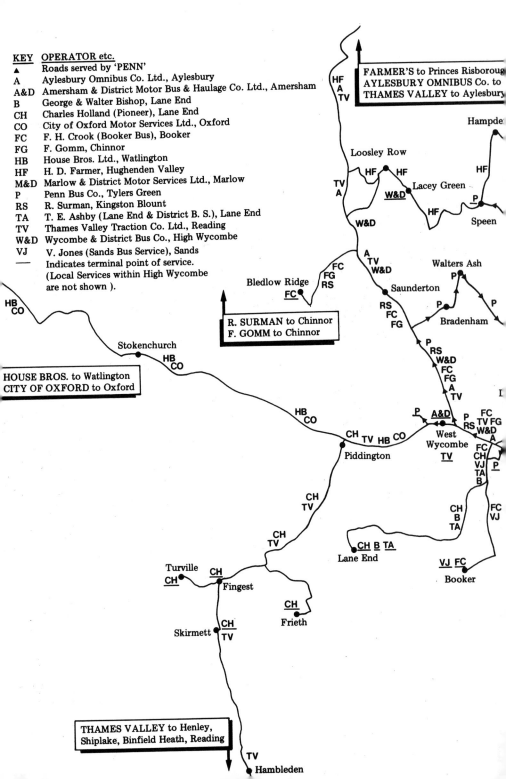

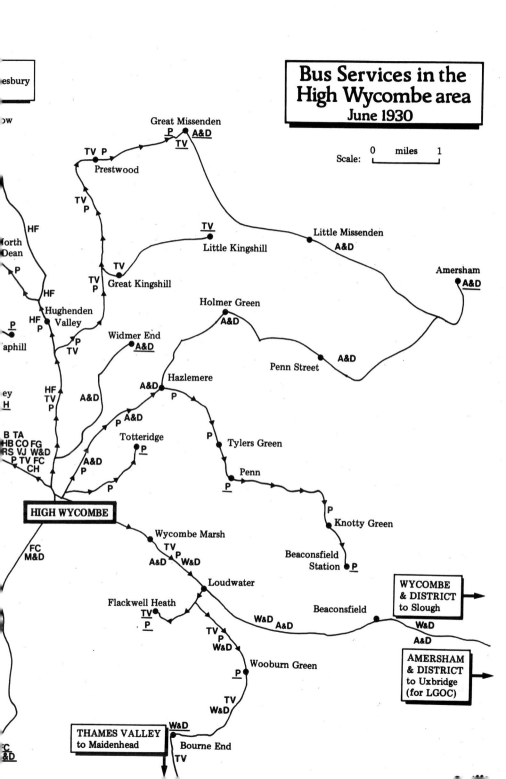

Only one example of the E-type Dennis was taken by 'Penn', though many more were to be found in High Wycombe in 'Amersham & District' livery. No. 19 (KX 1541) carried Strachan & Brown body which incorporated the front dash panel usually associated with this model.

High Wycombe-built Gilfords with bodies from the associated Wycombe Motor Bodies factory came into the fleet with No. 21 (KX 3484) in 1929. It is seen here at Wooburn Green in 1934 having been photographed by driver Stan Kilminster.

An 'Inspector's eye' view of the bus stands from the direction of the Frogmoor office. Beyond the fountain is a 'Penn' Gilford, whilst to the right, the 'Thames Valley' Inspector is busily erecting the excursions board in this early '30's view.

Further Wycombe-bodied Gilfords followed during 1930/1 and they were used widely on the busier routes. This view shows No. 23 (KX 5733) waiting to leave Frogmoor for Flackwell Heath. Note the large Gruss air-spring cylinders above the front bumper.

As more Gilfords entered service they also took over operation of the Penn route. No. 24 (KX 7382) was snapped by driver Kilminster en route shortly after delivery.

1932 saw a switch back to Dennis products, with 'Penn' taking a very early example of their new 'Lancet' model. No. 26 (KX 8092) was fairly unusual in having a Wycombe-built body, as the factory generally concentrated on coachwork for the associated Gilford chassis. No. 26 can be seen waiting for a journey to Penn on the Frogmoor stands. Note the old fountain, a significant feature of the island garden and a favourite meeting place.

No. 30 (APP 272) was amongst the 1934 intake of Dennis vehicles and carries a fine example of a Dennis-built bus body designed specifically to suit their 'Lancet 1' chassis.

Also part of the 1934 intake was 20-seater No. 31 (APP 273). Based on the newly-introduced 'Ace' chassis, it had a Dennis-built body which merged very well with the slightly awkward snout-like appearance of that model.

Further variety in Dennis models came with the purchase of 'Mace' No. 32 (BBH 755) in 1934, fitted with a 26-seat centre-doorway Dennis body which could also be used for Private Hire jobs which did not warrant a full-size vehicle.

Hat badges were made up of brass letters soldered to bands for inserting into the front of the peaked caps.

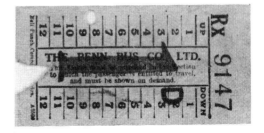

'Penn' used the commonplace Bell Punch tickets for its needs, this example being issued for a schoolboy's journey from Hazlemere to Wycombe in 1933 or 4.

"Streamline" coachwork was very much the mode in 1935, the raised rear windows and sweeping waistrail being typical means of achieving that look. No. 33 (BKX 431) was the first of the 'Penn' coaches with this style of coachwork and the first to be fitted with a radio.

The Dennis coach interiors were much in accordance with the trends of the mid-'30's, offering a blend of comfort and clean functional lines. This view shows the rearward view of the interior of No. 33 (BKX 431) - note the single seat adjacent to the sliding centre entrance.

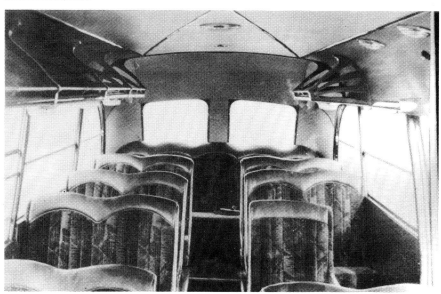

PENN BUS CO. FLEET LIST

No.	Reg. No.	Make & Model	Bodybuilder	Seats	New	Acq.	Sold	Remarks
-	BH 0311	Austin 2 ton	Coles	B20R	1/20		c 9/26	-
-	BH 5951	Ford 1-ton	Coles	B14R	7/20		c 8/26	-
-	(BH 9409)	Ford 1-ton	Coles	B14R	8/22		c 2/27	-
-	(BH 9991)	Ford 1-ton	Coles	B14R	3/23		c 2/27	-
1	PP 1194	Dennis 2½-ton	Strachan & Brown	B26R	1/24		by 8/35	-
2	PP 2245	Dennis 2½-ton	Strachan & Brown	B26R	7/24		8/35	to LPTB
3	PP 3006	Dennis 2½-ton	Strachan & Brown	B26R	1/25		by 8/35	-
4	PP 3005	Dennis2½-ton	Strachan & Brown	B26R	1/25		by 8/35	-
5	PP 3811	Dennis2½-ton	Strachan & Brown	B26R	4/25		by 8/35	-
6	PP 4616	Dennis 30 cwt	Strachan & Brown	B16R	7/25		3/29	-
7	PP 4875	Dennis 2½-ton	Strachan & Brown	B26R	10/25		8/35	to TV 278
8	PP 5166	Dennis 2½-ton	Strachan & Brown	B26R	12/25		8/35	to TV 279
9	PP 6811	Dennis 2½-ton	Strachan & Brown	B26R	8/26		by 8/35	-
10	PP 6918	Chevrolet X	? Coles	B14F	9/26		by 8/35	-
11	PP 7563	Chevrolet LM	Coles B14R	(ex Ford)	2/27		c 1/30	-
12	PP 7564	Chevrolet LM	Coles B14R	(ex Ford)	2/27		by 8/35	-
14	PP 9263	Dennis 2½-ton	Strachan & Brown	B26F	10/27		by 8/35	-
15	PP 8721	Dennis 2½-ton	Strachan & Brown	B26F	7/27		by 8/35	-
16	PP 9657	Leyland PLSC1	Strachan & Brown	B32F	1/28		8/35	to TV 280
17	KX 498	Dennis 2½-ton	Strachan & Brown	B26F	5/28		8/35	to TV 281
18	KX 1312	Dennis 2½-ton	Strachan & Brown	B26F	10/28		8/35	to TV 282
19	KX 1541	Dennis E	Strachan & Brown	B32R	12/28		8/35	to LPTB
20	KX 1734	Dennis 2½-ton	Strachan & Brown	B26F	1/29		8/35	to TV 283
21	KX 3484	Gilford 1660T	Wycombe	B32F	9/29		8/35	to TV 284
22	UV 7778	Gilford 1660T	Wycombe	B32F	/29	1/30	8/35	to LPTB
23	KX 5733	Gilford 1680T	Wycombe	B32F	9/30		8/35	to TV 285
24	KX 7382	Gilford 1680T	Wycombe	B32F	7/31		8/35	to TV 286
25	KX 7843	Gilford 1680T	Wycombe	C32F	12/31		8/35	to LPTB
26	KX 8092	Dennis Lancet	Wycombe	B32F	1/32		8/35	to TV 287
27	KX 8744	Dennis Lancet	Dennis	B32R	6/32		8/35	to TV 288
28	ABH 350	Dennis Lancet	Dennis	B32?	5/33		8/35	to LPTB
29	APP 271	Dennis Lancet	Dennis	C32F	5/34		8/35	to TV 289
30	APP 272	Dennis Lancet	Dennis	B32F	5/34		8/35	to TV 290
31	APP 273	Dennis Ace	Dennis	B20F	5/34		8/35	to TV 291
32	BBH 755	Dennis Mace	Dennis	B26C	12/34		8/35	to LPTB
33	BKX 431	Dennis Lancet	Dennis	C32C	3/35		8/35	to TV 292
34	BKX 696	Dennis Lancet	Dennis	B32C	5/35		8/35	to LPTB
35	BKX 898	Dennis Lancet	Dennis	C32C	5/35		8/35	to TV 293

Notes:-

Dennis 2½-tonners 2, 7 and 8 were rebodied Wycombe B26F in 1928.
Dennis 2½-tonner 15 was rebodied Strachan & Brown in 1/28 after a tree smashed the original body.
Gilford 22 was formerly a Gilford Motor Co. demonstrator.
Dennis 2½-ton No. 2 and Dennis E No. 19 did not receive LPTB fleet numbers.
Gilford's Nos. 22 and 25 became LPTB GF192 and GF191 (respectively).
Dennis 'Lancets' Nos. 28 and 34 became LPTB DT8B and DT9B, whilst 'Mace' No. 32 became LPTB DC3B.

terminus a short way westwards of the village to Chorley Road - this is also believed to be when the service between there and Wooburn Green was split at Frogmoor.

The other addition was a new route from Frogmoor to serve the growing population along the Bowerdean Road - High Wycombe seeing considerable housing development during the late 1920's and early 1930's.

Garaging for the expanding fleet was becoming a problem by 1927 and the original sheds were supplemented by a larger purpose-built structure. The old sheds continued in use for painting and cleaning, and even a bus washing machine was installed - though its use was later discontinued after the high-pressure water jets were found to be causing excessive rot!

The Borough Council had, however, grown somewhat tired of the numbers of complaints received about buses racing in the town and threatened both 'Penn' and 'Thames Valley' with the non-renewal of any of their licences in June 1927. Each Company replied blaming the other, leading Chepping Wycombe to even consider seeking powers to run its own buses as a part of a Bill it was then promoting through Parliament. As it was the Council did not become a direct operator of buses, but it did enter into an agreement with 'Thames Valley' which resulted in the October 1927 commencement of a new local service between Desborough Park Road and the King George V pub at Wycombe Marsh (via Dashwood Avenue, Green Street, Desborough Road, Newland Street, Castle Street and Totteridge Avenue), together with improved facilities between Frogmoor and Loudwater.

The above developments certainly strengthened the 'Valley's hand in the area, and that Company felt so bold as to approach Frederick Sugg that same month to make him an offer for his business!

However, the negotiations between the two parties came to nothing for several reasons. Firstly, Mr Sugg refused adamantly to reduce his asking price for the business and, secondly, 'Thames Valley' found that the 'London General' company had decided to give them notice that it would not be renewing the agreement relating to the Uxbridge services when the current one expired. This cast a shadow over future relations between TV and the LGOC which could well affect the Wycombe area, and against such a background, 'Thames Valley' did not persue its desire to buy 'Penn' out.

Increased loadings on some of the routes showed that some larger buses would be desirable and, with that in mind, Frederick Sugg visited the 1927 Commercial Motor Show where the forward-control Leyland 'Lion' PLSC1 model caught his eye. Such a layout meant that a 32-seater body could be fitted, so an order was place for one of that type.

'Thames Valley' had also been considering updating the stock at Wycombe and had allocated a number of new Tilling-Stevens saloons there during the Summer of 1927. 'Penn' driver Dick Cuff was quite attracted to the look of these buses and left to go on the 'Valley'. However, he soon found that they were also still fielding a considerable number of solid-tyred Thornycrofts as well, and was therefore rather relieved when he chanced to meet Frederick Sugg at Frogmoor one day and was offered his old job back!

The 'Penn' buses endeavoured to run in all the varied conditions the British weather could throw at them, and only two occasions are recalled when they failed to achieve that. During the severe winter of 1928/9 exceptionally heavy snowfalls blocked the lanes around the Tylers Green garage making it impossible for the buses to get out. Rather than waste the manpower at his disposal, Francis Sugg contacted the local Council and soon had his staff equipped and out clearing the road. They soon had a good stretch of road clear when, much to their annoyance, along came a 'Valley bus over the road they had just rendered passable! The other occasion involved a 'silver thaw' when everywhere was covered in ice. People trying to get about resorted to tieing rags to their hands and feet to crawl along or otherwise had to rely on holding onto fences and railings for support.

Ice also played its part in an accident that befell No. 9 on the Totteridge route. The bus was descending the very steep hill when ice was encountered, causing the bus to career back and forth from one side of the road to the other striking a number of lamp-standards on its way. The rearmost portion of the bodywork was knocked clean off when it caught a sturdy telegraph pole and was left laying in the road! Fortunately no passengers were injured in the process - though (ex-Guardsman) conductor Sid Henshaw had to restrain two frightened ladies from leaping from the moving vehicle. Generally though, the 'Penn' fleet did not meet with too many mishaps and when they did occur No. 15 was there to enhance its 'bogie bus' reputation!

As it was, No. 15 had already made itself conspicuous due to problems with its engine before the fateful day of its most spectactular mishap which occurred on the 6th January 1928. The bus was making its way past Pipers Corner on the Great Missenden route when a large tree was blown down and landed right across the bus and its unsuspecting occupants. The tree crashed through the wooden body and came to rest on the rear axle, but miraculously the five passengers and crew suffered no injuries other than a few cuts from broken glass. The bus was of the forward entrance layout and one passenger who had originally been sitting where the tree was to fall had just moved forward to speak to the crew and two passengers, thereby avoiding certain death. The two other passengers were at the extreme rear of the bus and were able to leave by way of the emergency exit in the centre of the rear of the bus, whilst conductor Ernie Orchard and driver Bill Dean and passengers at the front clambered out through the distorted front doorway.

Frederick and Francis Sugg and the Garage Foreman, Jesse Cadman attended the scene and a sawing gang from Plumridge's sawmill was called to the scene and they cut the massive trunk (all by hand using a two-man saw!) off at each side of the bus. The vehicle was then driven to the sawmill where a crane lifted off the remaining portion. Although the body was badly smashed, the chassis was found to be sound and Francis Sugg drove it to Acton the following day in order that Strachan & Brown could build a new body for it (the seats from the existing one being re-used).

One might have then reckoned that No. 15 had seen its share of woes, but unfortunately it went on to be involved in several fatal accidents - one when a driver reversed without the supervision of a conductor (as was Company policy), and another occasion when a man fell under the rear wheels when unsuccessfully attempting to board the bus as it rounded the corner of Castle Street.

On a happy note, January 1928 also saw the arrival of Leyland 'Lion' No. 16 (PP 9657). Strachan & Brown were once again the chosen bodybuilder and they constructed a front entrance bus body with seats for 32. Unfortunately, it was soon found that the 'Lion' was rather thirsty on petrol, and this somewhat cancelled out the economies offered by the increased seating capacity. It was also considered in due course that obtaining spare parts involved more work than had been the case with the Dennis vehicles. No. 16 therefore tended to be used on the Wooburn Green route, where there were no appreciable hill to tax its thirst.

A further two Dennis 2 1/2 tonners with front entrance 26-seat Strachan & Brown bodies were added to the fleet in 1928, becoming No. 17 (KX 498) in May and No. 18 (KX 1312) in October.

Also during 1928, three of the older Dennis buses were sent to the newly opened Wycombe Motor Bodies plant for rebodying. Buses 2, 7 and 8 were the trio treated to new 26-seat front entrance bodies, and the exercise certainly extended their working lives.

Chepping Wycombe Borough Council continued to be concerned about the dangers of traffice and congestion caused around the Frogmoor Gardens and, in November 1928, they introduced a one-way traffic scheme using the gardens as a central island.

Earlier that year though, both 'Penn' and 'Thames Valley' had sought legal opinion and had challenged the Council over whether it actually had the powers to regulate timetables etc. in the way that it had been increasingly inclined to do. It seems that the operators were advised that the Council could not force timetables upon them, but by then the whole matter of bus licencing had become such that the subject was taking up quite a lot of time and energy at the Ministry of Transport in the form of disputes between operators and licencing authorities over the interpretation of legislation (or lack of it).

During 1928 Frederick Sugg decided that the firm would benefit from the introduction of some younger management and he appointed Norman Hutchinson as Manager. However, this arrangement did not prove successful and Mr Hutchinson was replaced by Francis Sugg the following year.

Although the 'Lion' had been a bit of a disappointment, it was still considered desirable to persue the idea of larger capacity forward-control buses for use on the busier routes. 'Penn' once again turned to the Dennis range for its needs and took one of their E-type chassis fitted with a 32-seat rear entrance body by Strachan & Brown. It arrived in early December 1928 as No. 19 (KX 1541), and its arrival is believed to coincide with the commencement of the Flackwell Heath service (upon which it was usually to be found).

In fact no-one until then had dared to run a bus service up the steep Treadaway Hill leading up to Flackwell Heath from Loudwater. It remains impressive even today, but in those days of poorer road surfaces and brakes with less power than was desirable it posed a real danger indeed. The hill also had another obstacle on its length, that of a railway level crossing on the old Maidenhead to Wycombe line. Buses ascending the hill would sometimes have to halt for a train, leaving the bus driver with a difficult hill-start over the humps caused by the crossing having been built on the level in a slight cutting into the hillside. Drivers coming down the hill had a tough enough job bringing their charges to a steady stop at the base of the hill without having to contend with a stop at the crossing gates further up.

Flackwell Heath therefore became one of the last destinations to which the 'Penn' routes expanded, the other late addition being a service up to Totteridge. The latter route involved using the steep and narrow Totteridge Lane and so 'Little Dennis' No. 6 was used on that run, road improvements on the Speen route by then making it possible to run the 26-seaters there. Quite when Totteridge was reached is uncertain, but it was sometime during late '28 or early '29.

Local road imrovements continued to take place as the new residential areas around the outskirts of Wycombe were developed, and little No. 6's pioneering days were brought to a close with its disposal in March 1929.

Shortly before that, in January of that year, the last in a long line of Dennis 2 1/2 tonners was placed in service as No. 20 (KX 1734). As with the more recent examples, it carried a front entrance 26-seat body built by Strachan & Brown and was purchased to replace No. 6 (though it was generally No. 9 which covered the Totteridge route).

In the meantime the 'Uxbridge Special Area Agreement' between 'Thames Valley' and 'London General' had come to a close on 31st December 1928, resulting in the LGOC making arrangements with the 'Amersham & District' Company (in which it held a considerable interest) to operate certain routes in the Wycombe area. This change led to A&D outstationing some buses at the 'Thames Valley' Wycombe Marsh garage until a new LGOC-funded garage could be built at the bottom of Marlow Hill, the arrangement lasting from March to December 1929. 'Thames Valley' lost its Uxbridge to Amersham route and also the Chalfont St Peter to Windsor run under the new arrangements, whilst the change also saw the 'Valley buses replaced by those of A&D on the Holmer Green and Penn service. The existing local service between the King George V and Desborough Park Road became a joint operation between TV and A&D, in recognition of the LGOC's claim to a stake in the Wycombe area, whilst the buses between

19

Uxbridge and West Wycombe were looked after by the 'General' itself from the Uxbridge (Denham Road) garage which it had taken back from 'Thames Valley'.

Fortunately for 'Penn', it was found to be much easier to get along with the Amersham company than with their arch-rivals the 'Valley', and no squabbling occurred over the short stretches of route common to both firms between Wycombe and Penn village. Good relations existed with the A & D Manager, Bill Randall, whilst their Garage Manager, Mr Knowles was actually the brother of 'Penn' driver, George Knowles. Indeed, as both firms had very similar vehicles (even to the choice of bodybuilders!) there were even occasions when they would help each other out with spare parts.

It will be recalled that three of the older Dennis buses had been to the Wycombe Motor Bodies works for new bodies during 1928, that particular firm having been set up as a subsidiary of the Gilford Motor Co. in addition to its chassis production line at its new home in Wycombe. As it widely known, Gilford did not manufacture the parts for their chassis, but rathermore assembled proprietory items to produce designs that were both powerful and forward-looking. Most of the passenger chassis built were fitted with the American-built 6-cylinder Lycoming engine, whilst there were other refinements to be found such as air suspension on the front axle.

It was therefore only natural than 'Penn' should be tempted into taking an interest in these vehicles being made on its very doorstep, and No. 21 (KX 3484) was the first in a number of forward-control Gilford chassis with Wycombe-built bodies to be purchased. It had a 32-seater front entrance bus body and arrived in September 1929, its usual duty being the Wooburn Green route.

Working hours were long in those days and a 'normal' working week was around the 80-hour mark, but as that was widespread practice busmen did not feel particularly put upon.

Following the dismissal of Norman Huchinson, Francis Sugg (aged 18) had become Manager and set about taking stock of the Company's performance. His youthful rise to such a position posed a query as to what he should wear to mark his status - the matter being settled as a dark suit, bowler hat and spats!

Unfortunately though, Francis soon found himself having to deal with a brief strike caused by some over-zealous reporting of minor incidents by the 'Penn' Inspector. All was back to rights after one day, and the usual good relations between the management, the men and the T&GWU were soon restored. Frederick Sugg actively supported the idea of Union representation for his employees, even to the extent of insisting on a closed-shop from about 1931. Later, after the Company was sold, he received a letter from the local T&GWU official praising him for the good working relations he had fostered.

On the vehicle front, another Gilford similar to the first was acquired in January 1930. This was registered UV 7778 and had served as a demonstrator for the Gilford concern in 1929 before coming to 'Penn' as their No. 22

The Borough Council was keen to see more buses out to West Wycombe and managed to persuade the 'Valley' to extend its local service westwards in early 1930. This venture proved to be un-remunerative and was consequently withdrawn in October of that year. However, with the pending legislation of the Road Traffic Act (1930) in mind, 'Thames Valley' also sought permission to run buses from Wycombe to Naphill and Speen, but the Council refused on the grounds that the 'Penn' services were adequate.

'Penn' itself sought permission during June 1930 for an extension of its Bowerdean Road service on to Totteridge via the Bowerdean Road extension and Totteridge Hill. This was refused at that time on the recommendation of the Borough Surveyor, who considered the roads as yet unfit for bus traffic. Not long afterwards though, the necessary works were completed and buses thereafter ran to Totteridge via that route.

The fleet had been growing steadily since its modest beginning in 1920 and, as of June 1930 consisted of the following: Dennis 2-and-a-half tonners Nos. 1, 2, 3, 4, 5, 7, 8, 9, 14, 15, 17, 18 and 20; Chevrolet 14-seaters Nos. 10, 11 and 12; Leyland 'Lion' No. 16; Dennis E-type No. 19; and Gilfords Nos. 21 and 22.

A third Gilford bus arrived in September 1930 in the shape of No. 23 (KX 5733), once again carrying a Wycombe-built 32-seat front entrance body.

Two more Gilfords were added during 1931, bus No. 24 (KX 7382) being delivered in July and No. 25 following in December. The latter was the first vehicle to be purchased with coach bodywork though the Wycombe bus bodies were to a high standard

21

internally) and it carried a 32-seat front entrance body built at the Wycombe plant. Its purchase reflected Francis Sugg's conviction that 'Penn' should enter the Private Hire field in earnest to improve the Company's less than rosy financial position. Such work had to be sought in the areas surrounding Wycombe, as the market had been well covered by both the 'Valley' and 'Pilot Coaches' in the town for some time. As further Gilfords came into use they also took over the operation of the Wycombe to Penn route.

However, 1931 is more importantly recalled as the year in which the effects of the 1930 Road Traffic Act were felt. 'Penn' very wisely did not leave itself at the reliance of local representation over this new and wide-ranging legislation, but engaged the services of Mr J.R. Cort Bathurst (a solicitor of Chancery Lane specialising in matters relating to road transport law).

At the Traffic Commissioners session held to cover the Wycombe area applications for the new Road Service Licences the Commissioner Sir Reginald Ford found that 'Penn', 'Thames Valley' and 'Amersham & District' had all counter-objected to each others proposals. He told all three parties to go to another room and to sort out between themselves who was going to apply for what - otherwise he would not issue any of the licences to any of them! The result was that each firm then applied for licences only for the services they were already operating, and this left 'Penn' receiving licences for all of its existing routes. The only concession forced upon it by the Commissioner was that both it and the 'Valley' were required to produce a joint timetable and make tickets interavailable on the Wycombe to Great Missenden service.

As already noted Private Hire had been more vigorously pursued since Francis Sugg had taken over as Manager, and the Company managed to increase its share of the local market and therefore offset some of the losses then being incurred on the bus side. Most of the problem related to lack of programmed maintenance which led to breakdowns and hurried journeys to collect spare parts. Francis then arranged a spare parts store and instituted a programme of regular overhauls which soon showed its worth.

Another facet of this reorganisation was the registering, on 7th April 1931, of the Company as a re-titled 'Penn Bus Company Limited', the sole shareholders being Frederick and Alice Sugg. Frederick was the Managing Director, whilst Francis then became Manager and Secretary.

The next vehicle to arrive was No. 26 (KX 8092), and it heralded a return to Dennis products once again. It arrived in January 1932 and was based on the newly-introduced 'Lancet 1' model, being only the 8th production example supplied. A link with the Wycombe Motor Bodies Co. was, however, retained as they were responsible for the 32-seat front entrance bus body it carried. The chassis had actually been delivered by Dennis direct to the 'Penn' garage, and this caused the latter a slight problem in getting it to the bodyworks due to not being in possession of any 'trade plates'. So Francis Sugg had to take the chassis on a chilly early-morning run using only the back roads in order to avoid being spotted by the Police!

Although the Gilfords were undoutedly fast machines, they could be a bit heavy on petrol when used on the busy local services and this led to a return to the more conservative products of the Dennis factory in order to assist with the economies then being sought.

A second 'Lancet 1' arrived in June 1932 but this example carried a 32-seat rear entrance bus body built by Dennis themselves, the factory having made a return to bodybuilding after a period of relying on others for that side of the business. This was bus No. 27 and it was registered KX 8744.

The fleet had been steadily increasing, with only a small number of withdrawals occurring in the earlier years. As already noted, the little Fords had been replaced by Chevrolets, whilst the older Dennis buses had been switched to other new or rural routes as the larger types took their places on the more heavily-trafficked services. Some thinning of the ranks did occur in the early '30's, though full dates etc. are unfortunately lacking. What is known is that the following were ousted as new vehicles came into stock between June 1930 and August 1935:- Dennis buses Nos. 1, 9, 14 and 15 and the three Chevrolets. (No. 10 having been used on the Beaconsfield Station run until at least June 1932).

The advent of the 1930 Act had effectively brought to an end both the expansion of services and the fierce rivalry with the 'Valley', but a new worry loomed on the horizon for the Suggs in the form of the London Passenger Transport Bill, which sought to provide the proposed London Passenger Transport Board with a monopoly of operation within its designated area. That area also included the eastern part of the 'Penn' empire and Frederick Sugg foresaw this threat as one likely to put him out of business - a fact all the more galling after having prevailed against the resources of 'Thames Valley' for so long!

Although it brought little real comfort to the Suggs, the formation of the LPTB in July 1933 did not immediately result in the loss of any routes by 'Penn' - the Board having more pressing matters to deal with elsewhere.

1933 remained a somewhat cautious year at 'Penn' and only one bus was purchased. Again it was a Dennis 'Lancet 1' with a 32-seat body by their own coachbuilders, although the entrance position remains unconfirmed. Bus No. 28 was registered ABH 350 and was placed in service during May of that year.

Indeed, even before the LPTB had come into being, there had been a joint approach by the LGOC and the Amersham Company for the purchase of 'Penn'. The negotiations had come to nothing, due to what they considered too high an asking price, but they certainly aroused the interest of the 'Thames Valley' Board, who were themselves a little apprehensive about the future of their own operations in the Wycombe area under the pending legislation.

The 1930 Act had already very much polarised the routes in the area, leading 'Thames Valley' to approach a number of local operators with a view to buying them out during the 1933/4 period - though success was very limited as most operators wanted to hold out for a good price.

'Thames Valley' did manage to extend its Local Service to the King George V onto Loudwater and Flackwell Heath, despite strong objections from 'Penn', whilst their other Local Service was altered to have some journeys running to Bowerdean Road instead of the King George V - both revisions taking effect from 1st January 1933.

'Penn's' own Locals continued to evolve to suit the gradual expansion of the built-up Wycombe area, and the Desborough Park Road route had been extended onto Mill End Road (via Eaton Avenue) by August 1933.

Sometime between that date and early 1935 route numbers were allocated to each service for timetable purposes but these were not displayed on the buses themselves.

The year 1934 saw 4 new Dennis vehicles entering service, 3 of them arriving during May. These became Nos. 29, 30 and 31 (APP 271, 272 and 273) but each was distinctly different from the other. No. 29 was another "Lancet 1', but this time with a 32-seat front entrance coach body built by Dennis, whilst No. 30 was a bus-bodied

24

'Lancet 1' with a 32-seat front entrance body from the same factory. No.31 was, however, based on the newly-introduced normal-control 'Ace' chassis and carried a 20-seat front entrance bus body built also by Dennis. It was used on bus work but evidently also saw use for smaller Private Hire parties, and it also had the distiction of being only the third production example of the 'Ace' built.

One of the newest 'Lancets' was used for a particularly notable Private Hire during September 1934, when it provided the transport from the Wycombe Church to Flackwell Heath for the wedding guests of driver 'Gypsy' Smith and his bride Jessie.

Other jobs were for various religious organisations and Women's Institutes, etc. the Salvation Army, plus the annual runs to the very popular Aldershot Tattoo and Ascot Races (both of which were held at much the same dates during June).

As mentioned before, Frederick Sugg had developed a good relationship with the people at the Dennis factory, hence his willing-ness to take an example of new models as they were released, but he still used his powers of persuasion to twist their arm a little to keep the price down and/or get 'extras' included at no additional cost!

During the last month of 1934 a further variety of Dennis chassis was added to the fleet in the shape of No. 32 (BBH 755), an example of the forward-control 'Mace' which had recently been introduced as an alternative to the 'Ace'. It carried a 26-seat Dennis-built centre entrance bus body, and although built largely to the service bus standards of the day, the sliding door shows that it was also intended for Private Hire work as well. Indeed, the Dennis interiors of that era were finished to a high standard, making it quite feasible to use those vehicles as widely as possible.

Determined to maintain the momentum already achieved on the local coaching front, 'Penn' placed a further order with Dennis Bros. for a pair of 'Lancet 1' chassis to be fitted with the latest style of streamlined coachwork in readiness for the 1935 'season'. After the order had been laid down, it came to Francis Sugg's attention that the three Leyland 'Tigers' then on order by 'Thames Valley' for use at Wycombe were to be fitted with the latest coaching refinement -radio! He and his father lost no time in contacting the coachworks manager at Dennis and arranged to have radios installed in the two 'Lancets' which were nearing completion. The outcome was that 'Penn' got the first of its 'Lancets' delivered two weeks before the 'Valley 'Tigers' arrived from Duples. Just to bring the message fully home to potential passengers, the first of the 'Penn' radio coaches was placed on public display (with radio on) at Frogmoor shortly after it arrived in March - quite what TV's Traffic Manager, J W Dally, said when he heard what had happened has not been recorded for posterity!

The 'Radio Coaches' became Nos. 33 and 35 (BKX 431 and BKX 898) and both carried 32-seat centre entrance bodies, No. 35 having arrived towards the end of April. The intervening vehicle was No. 34 (BKX 696) and was another bus-bodied 'Lancet 1'. Again the body was by Dennis and seated 32, but this example had a centre entrance layout and it took to the road at the end of March 1935.

These three 'Lancets' were actually the last vehicles to be purchased by 'Penn' as serious consideration needed to be given to the fresh overtures being made by 'Thames Valley' regarding a possible takeover. Indeed, the 'Valley' had already been discussing the topic of 'Penn' with the LPTB, some of the routes being within the latter's designated area. Between themselves they had agreed that TV would put forward an offer to 'Penn' of £29,000 for the whole undertaking, and that the LPTB would then buy certain assets off them for £13,750. The LPTB share of the spoils would include the Tylers Green garage, three routes and approximately one-third of the fleet.

The LPTB had of course continued to be most active in acquiring bus operators throughout its area since the 1933 Act, including the routes of the larger firms where appropriate, and Frederick Sugg therefore considered it better to sell his operations voluntarily and as a whole rather than eventually lose three profitable routes to the Board.

Negotiations between 'Thames Valley' and 'Penn' were brought to a conclusion in July 1935 and a takeover date of 1st August agreed. The three routes within the LPTB area were immediately handed over to them for operation, and they comprised:

High Wycombe - Terriers - Hazlemere - Tylers Green - Penn (Post Office); Tylers Green - Penn (Church) - Saucy Corner - Knotty Green - Beaconsfield Station; and High Wycombe - Totteridge.

The garage passed into the hands of the Board, as did the following vehicles : (LPTB fleet numbers, where allocated, as shown in the Fleet List)

26

No. 2 PP 2245 Dennis 2 1/2 ton   No. 28 ABH 350 Dennis 'Lancet 1'
No. 19 KX 1541 Dennis E   No. 32 BBH 755 Dennis 'Mace'
No. 22 UV 7778 Gilford 1660T   No. 34 BKX 696 Dennis 'Lancet 1'
No. 25 KX 7843 Gilford 1680T

Dennis No. 2 and the E-type were soon withdrawn by the Board, whereas the two Gilfords and the pair of 'Lancets' lasted until 1937 and the 'Mace' until 1938.

All of the existing 85 employees were offered employment with either the LPTB or 'Thames Valley', agreement having already been reached that the longer-service men would be offered positions with the Board as its Pay & Conditions were better than those offered by TV. However, although most were suitably accommodated by the new owners, a few did leave rather than work for their old arch-rivals.

'Thames Valley' took over all of the other routes, some of which largely paralleled its own, together with the Private Hire aspects of the business. Some operations, such as the Great Missenden, Flackwell Heath routes and some Local Services were assimilated into the TV services which already existed, whilst the following were additional routes formed from the takeover:

Route 31 High Wycombe - West Wycombe - Bradenham - Walters Ash - Naphill
Route 32 High Wycombe - West Wycombe (Chorley Road)
Route 33 Frogmoor - Desborough Park Road - Eaton Avenue - Mill End Road
Route 34 High Wycombe - Hughenden - North Dean - Speen

Incidentally, the existing Local Service (Route 26) continued to be operated jointly by TV/LPTB after the takeover and division of 'Penn', operating between the King George V, Wycombe Marsh, New Bowerdean Road, Duke Street, Green Street, Desborough Park Road and Mill End Road.

An order for 16 Leyland 'Tiger' TS7 single-deck buses was soon placed by TV as replacements for the same number of vehicles taken over from 'Penn', although delivery was not possible until December 1935 Some of the ex-'Penn' vehicles were not used at all by 'Thames Valley', other buses being drafted into Wycombe from the Summer surplus of buses kept to cover the busy Ascot Race Week period. Some vehicles did see service with the new owners, notably the 'Lancet' coaches which were used to cover existing commitments on excursion and Private Hire work. Indeed, the latter so impressed the TV Chief Engineer Basil Sutton that he seriously thought of ordering some more for the coach fleet - but the idea was dropped after one disgraced itself with a breakdown on a trip to the coast at the August Bank Holiday!

The vehicles taken over by 'Thames Valley' were as follows: (all were given TV fleet numbers whether run or not, and these can be found in the Fleet List);

Dennis 2 1/2 tonners Nos. 7 (PP4875), 8 (PP 5166), 17 (KX 498), 18 (KX 1312) and 20 (KX 1734); Leyland 'Lion' PLSC1 No. 16 (PP9657); Gilford 1660T No. 21 (KX 3484); Gilford 1680T's No. 23 (KX 5733) and No. 24 (KX 7382); Dennis 'Lancets' Nos. 26 (KX 8092), 27 (KX 8744), 29 (APP 271), 30 (APP 272), 33 (BKX 431) and 35 (BKX 898); and Dennis 'Ace' No. 31 (APP 273).

Also taken over by TV was the office at 35 Frogmoor, which continued to serve as an enquiries and parcels office for many more years.

Frederick Sugg then continued his 'retirement' (he was by then aged 76!), whilst Francis was employed by 'Thames Valley' as Traffic Superintendent at their Wycombe Marsh garage (as second-in-charge under Ernest Jeffries, himself coming to TV with the takeover of 'Marlow & District'). Francis remained there, assisting with the absorption of the former 'Penn' routes, until the end of 1935 when he was offered the chance to take charge of the TV operations at Maidenhead. However, his mother had recently passed away and his father's agedness meant that he did not wish to move to Maidenhead so he declined the offer and went to join another family member in the furniture trade instead.

Frederick Sugg lived to the age of 85 and passed away in 1944, whilst Francis's various business ventures kept him busily engaged until he too finally retired when well into his 70's.

That the 'Penn Bus Company' is still recalled, by so many local people and with such affection, for its courteous and efficient service to the public serves as a creditable remembrance of all those who made it the success it certainly was!

28